D0471072

Dogs

Dog Care
Puppy Care
How To Take Care Of
And Train
Your Dog Or Puppy

By Ace McCloud
Copyright © 2014

Disclaimer

Table of Contents

Be sure to check out my website for all my Books and Audio books.

www.AcesEbooks.com

Introduction

I want to thank you and congratulate you for buying the book, "Dogs: Dog Care-Puppy Care- How To Take Care Of And Train Your Dog or Puppy."

A dog or a puppy is a great choice for a pet. It is said that a dog is "man's best friend." They are domestic animals that are similar to humans and have been a favorite companion for humanity for hundreds of years. Dogs make great pets for many reasons. They are almost always happy to see you, they provide a great source of unconditional love and they have been known to bring incredible joy into the lives of their owners. Dogs are great for sharing feelings of happiness and promoting healing and support. They are also some of the most cute and cuddly creatures that you may ever see. For the most part, dogs make great family pets because they tend to get along well with kids, they can be trained and they can live a fairly long time.

A dog can also be a great learning tool in addition to being a great friend. Many families divide the responsibilities of taking care of a dog and use it to instill responsibility in their young children. A dog can also motivate you to go outside and get some fresh air and exercise. Dogs are loyal, happy, fun and will certainly become part of your family in no time.

That being said, adding a dog to your family also means taking on a great responsibility. Unlike cats, which can often take care of themselves with minimal assistance, your dog will rely on you for many things. It is up to you to take care of it, feed it, keep it healthy and keep it occupied. You will also have to devote some time and patience to training and getting your dog on track for good behavior. You will have to take it to the vet and exercise it regularly. There is also a great deal of consideration that you need to make before you actually decide to get a dog. Since there are so many different breeds, all of which have different attitudes, requirements and temperaments, it is important that you really think about your decision carefully.

Preparing to get a dog and working on making it a great addition to your home can be one of the most worthwhile things that you ever do. This book will guide you with the best information and strategies available that will allow you to make great decisions when it comes to choosing and caring for your new friend. You will also discover all of the pros and cons when it comes to the most common breeds as well as learning about the best ways to train, feed, groom and take care of your dog or puppy. This book aims to serve as your hand-guide to helping your dog become a permanent and happy member of your family. If you have not yet bought a dog or puppy, the first chapter will guide you through making that critical decision. If you've already bought your dog, the rest of this book will cover great training methods, nutritional information, playtime ideas and much more that will help you and your dog live a happy life together!

Chapter 1: How To Choose The Right Dog Or Puppy

Unlike some other pets, choosing a dog requires a great deal of consideration and research before you come to a decision. There are many different types of dogs to choose from and they have different levels of needs and attention. Dogs are not like cats, hamsters, goldfish, or just any other critter where you can leave them with some food and water and they'll be able to care for themselves. The average lifespan of a dog is between 10 and 13 years, so when choosing a dog, you must remind yourself that you will be making a long-term commitment. It can be tempting to go out and get one a whim or because your friend or family member got one and you just love it so much you want one of your own. However, if you don't do your research, you may end up with more than you can handle.

The Most Popular Breeds

Retrievers (Golden or Labrador). A retriever dog often comes with the mildest of tempers and will play catch with you for hours, hence its "retriever" name. Retrievers also love water and they will go swimming with you or play games where you throw toys into the water and they will go get them. The only downside of these dogs is that you must watch their diets carefully, as they can tend to overeat. These types of dogs are great for families with small kids and they are not likely to bite hard unless they have food in their mouth. Another downside is that some retrievers are very hairy and shed easily, so you may need to groom them often. Golden retrievers have long hair.

German Shepherds. German shepherds are big dogs that can come off with a tough demeanor, best known for being guard dogs, but they can be sweet and loving as well. When trained, these types of dogs can get along well with all ages. It is very important to consider how much time you can dedicate to training a German shepherd, because if not trained it can become aggressive and uncontrollable. Due to their big size and energy levels, German shepherds require a good amount of exercise and living space. In terms of health, these dogs are inclined to hip dysplasia, digestive problems, or skin problems. They can also make good guard dogs, as I vividly remember as a child when I would zoom by the house with the scary German shepherd in it, who would always love to run out to the edge of his chain and bark at me.

Beagle. Beagles are adorable, wonderful, medium-sized dogs that are world-renowned for their ability to track scents, making them excellent hunting dogs. They come in a variety of colors, but their most common color scheme is tri-colored (brown, white, and black). Beagles make great friends and their hair is short, so they don't need to be brushed too often. They are also very energetic, leading to their #1 drawback—their sense of smell. Once a beagle gets a whiff of something it likes, that is all that it will focus on. This can be especially evident at the dinner table. Their powerful sense of smell also makes it difficult to train beagles as they sometimes will run away due to their curiosity and hunting instincts. They also tend to bark and howl a lot. However, beagles are good with children and can be extremely friendly.

Yorkshire Terrier. Yorkshire Terriers are little dogs that you might often see in someone's lap. They make good companions as they love to snuggle up with you as you engage in something that is non-active, such as watching tv, reading, or napping. These shy dogs are loyal to those who they are familiar with and can often feel timid around other dogs. One downside of having a Yorkshire terrier is that they like to "yap" constantly, which may be problematic if you have close neighbors. While these dogs should be allowed to roam around the house, they do not require extensive exercise, making them good options for senior citizens who are in need of a pal.

Bulldog. Bulldogs give off an intimidating demeanor but they can actually be sweet and loyal to their owners. The unfortunate part about bulldogs is that they are more inclined to suffer from a slew of health issues, bringing their lifespan down from 10 to 6 years. Nearly 90% of bulldogs develop hip dysplasia as well as suffer from depression. If you are considering getting a bulldog as a pet, you should consult with your vet to learn more about how you can provide it with the best care.

Border Collie. Border collies are smart, loving dogs that come packed with an insane amount of energy. Due to their high energy levels, it is important that anyone who considers getting a border collie calculate how much space and exercise they can provide for it. If you do not allow a border collie to release its energy, it could, in turn, begin to tear up your house. On the flip side, research shows that border collies are easily trainable due to their high levels of intelligence. Border collies also come with their share of basic health issues but overall rank as pretty durable.

Poodle. Poodles are incredibly smart dogs that are very easy to train and teach tricks. They come in 3 different sizes—large, miniature and toy, which gives you some options compared to the size of your home. Their coats are pretty thin and they don't shed as much, which makes them good pets for those who have allergies or who don't want fur all over the house. Out of all purebred dogs, Poodles are the least likely to have health problems. In addition to being smart, they are also very energetic and require a good deal of exercise. The only real drawback to a Poodle is that they are geared more towards women than men due to their stereotypical "girlish" appearance. However, there is a guy in my neighborhood who loves walking around with his beautiful black and white poodles all the time.

Dachshund. Dachshunds are friendly, curious dogs that are famously known for their "hot dog" shape. Their energy levels are medium but it is important to keep a dachshund busy, as it likes to explore and can sometimes get into trouble.

Their coats can either be smooth, wiry, or long. On the downside, dachshunds can be a little harder to train due to their stubborn nature.

Rottweiler. Rottweilers are probably best known for their tough, aggressive and intimidating demeanor. While they may be regarded as dangerous dogs, they tend to only act aggressively when not well-trained. With the right kind of training, a Rottweiler can make a great all-around dog. If you do consider choosing a Rottweiler as your dog, it is important to take its strength and temperament into mind. Rottweilers can get nervous around strangers, so if you have a lot of people coming in and out of your house, you may want to rethink getting a Rottweiler as a pet. On the bright side, Rottweilers do not tend to have as many health issues as other dogs.

Doberman Pinscher. Doberman Pinschers are medium to large -sized dogs that pack a fearless, alert personality. They are best known for being strong and powerful companions who can make good watch dogs. One of the best things about this type of dog is that it is very easy to train and its coat is smooth, making it easy to maintain. Since Doberman pinschers are so strong and powerful, it is vital that you be able to exercise them regularly. My friend in college had a big Doberman Pinscher named "Duke." He never actually bit anyone, but boy could he be scary when he wanted to be! After my first encounter with him all alone, I went to the pet store to get him some treats for the next time we met! Later on I had great fun going on my runs with him around the neighborhood.

Siberian Husky. Siberian Huskies are medium-sized, friendly, gentle dogs who were originally bred to work in packs. Though they can come off as intimidating, they are actually very warm dogs who will get along well with children. In terms of their coat, these types of dogs require weekly brushing at the minimum due to their thick, double coat. On the plus side, Siberian huskies do not have that "dog" smell like other dogs do, so you will not have to worry about any odors.

German Pointer. German shorthaired pointers are big dogs with a scary demeanor, but under that is a sweet, gentle soul. These types of dogs grow to be very large and thus come with a lot of energy. It is very important that you be able to provide a German shorthaired pointer with plenty of exercise and love, otherwise it is more likely to develop anxiety problems. In terms of health, these dogs tend to be healthier than other breeds.

Shih Tzu. Shih Tzu's are toy dogs that tend to be friendly, extroverted and affectionate. They get along good with their owners as well as those who they are not as familiar with, making them a great family pet. Shih Tzu's grow to be about 10 inches long, making them good dogs for small homes. Shih Tzu's also have long ears and curly little tails, making them very cute and adorable. Their coats are thick and silk-like. One drawback of getting a Shih Tzu is that its thick fur requires constant brushing. Shih Tzu's are also more inclined to have health problems such as dysplasia, breathing problems and liver issues.

Great Dane. Great Danes are large dogs that are strong, friendly and noble. Though they are not usually aggressive, they still make great watch dogs due to their large size and demeanor. Their coats are short and do not require extensive grooming. Furthermore, this type of dog gets along well with children and adults of all ages. The only drawback is that you must closely watch their health due to their large size and appetite.

Boxer. Some people choose a boxer as an alternative to a Rottweiler because they are similar in size and demeanor but much friendlier and less anxious. Boxers share the Rottweiler's bonus of being healthy; however, boxers can be a little more challenging to train. It is best to start training a boxer from a puppy to ensure leadership. Finally, a boxer requires a large amount of space. Another great thing about boxers is their short hair, which doesn't tend to shed all over. Finally, boxers will be protective of younger kids, which is fine as long as they do not think the children are in harm's way—otherwise, a boxer may act out aggressively.

Greyhound. Greyhounds are large, gentle and mildly energetic dogs that make great house dogs. Though they do enjoy a little bit of run time, Greyhounds are mostly mellow. They can be fairly difficult to train but it is doable. Their short, smooth coats only require occasional brushing. Overall, the Greyhound is a noble dog that can make a great pet.

Chihuahua. Chihuahuas are small dogs who have the tendency to either be extremely loyal or extremely aggressive. I am sure you can think to a time where you've seen someone's Chihuahua go crazy or you may have seen one's temperament depicted on TV. Due to their unpredictable behavior, this type of dog may not be a good option if you have small kids. On the other hand, it might be a great fit for an older adult who has no other companions. The only drawbacks to getting a Chihuahua are its health issues, which can include seizures or hypoglycemia. They can also tend to bark a lot.

Pug. Pugs are similar to bulldogs in that they also share a slew of health issues. Most significantly, pugs tend to have breathing issues due to the shape of their face, leading many owners to actually have to pay to get their pugs' faces reconstructed just so they can get more air. On the bright side, pugs can be very cute and there are breeders who are working on ways to re-breed them to avoid breathing issues.

Boston Terrier. Boston terriers are small dogs that are friendly, trainable and very adaptable. These types of dogs are best known for being able to live in any type of setting, especially large cities. Their coats are short and sleek, making the Boston terrier a dog that is easy to maintain. Their energy levels tend to be medium. Boston terriers love to go on walks and they are always up for play time. They are good family dogs.

Mastiff. The Mastiff is a large dog that can come off as strong and courageous, but with a gentle demeanor on the inside. Their coats are short and smooth which does not require extensive grooming but it is important that you keep the wrinkles on their head clean. Their energy levels are medium and they often enjoy a good, long walk. These types of dogs make good family pets. In terms of health issues, it is important to watch their weight, as these dogs can tend to overeat.

Dalmatian. Dalmatians, best known for being firehouse dogs and the stars of major movies, are medium-sized dogs that are loyal, intelligent and affectionate. Despite their cute nature, these dogs are bred with a great stamina, making them good partners for those who are really active. They can become anxious around strangers, but all in all they make good family pets. Their coats are short and sleek and only require occasional brushing and combing.

Jack Russell Terrier. Jack Russell Terriers are energetic, curious, and friendly dogs who need a good amount of exercise and playtime. These types of dogs make good pets for those who have a very active lifestyle. Their coats are often smooth or rough and only require occasional grooming. Overall, they are confident dogs that make good pets all around.

Maltese. Maltese dogs are little, charming and best known for their long, white hair. Due to their long hair, these types of dogs do require extensive grooming. Maltese dogs have a medium energy level and enjoy walks and playtime but they also make good lap dogs. Overall, these dogs are friendly and fairly easy to train. They can also make a good watch dog with their powerful, determined bark.

Cocker Spaniel. Cocker spaniels are small to medium-sized dogs that are very friendly to nearly everyone. Though they are loved for their friendly nature, there are a few downsides to getting a cocker spaniel. First and foremost, they are more challenging to train. They are also prone to many health issues, such as ear and eye problems. On the bright side, cocker spaniels have very soft, beautiful fur that is perfect for petting and snuggling. These types of dogs can make good lap dogs.

Welsh Corgi. Welsh Corgis are small dogs that are friendly, energetic, and bold. They are known as herding dogs as many farmers use them to herd cattle. Welsh Corgis make good lap dogs but they require extensive brushing due to their thick fur. They are fairly easy to train and often make good guard dogs due to their strong bark.

There are many more great types of dogs that you can consider. If I listed them all, I would need to write two books! Check out justdogbreed.com to see a complete list of the most popular breeds and dogbreedinfo.com for a complete list of all breeds. There are many different breeds to choose from, so it is very important to do as much research as possible to find the right dog for you and/or your family.

Things To Research and Consider

In addition to picking a breed, there are some other factors that you should consider when picking out a new dog or puppy.

Costs. Costs are one of the most important things to think about when you're looking at getting a dog. You will need to put out money for vet bills, food, toys, and anything else your dog may need (bedding, leashes, dog houses, etc). Consider the difference between purebreds and mutts. With a purebred, you are bound to experience more health issues which can add up in costs.

Energy Levels. As you have learned, the majority of dogs have high to medium energy levels which require regular exercise or play time. This is an important factor to consider for yourself. What is your physical condition like? Do you exercise regularly? Ask yourself questions related to whether you could support your dog's energy requirements. If you are not in good health or able to keep up with an energetic dog or if you don't have a big backyard, you might want to consider getting a smaller dog.

The Size of the Dog. One of the most important factors that you must consider is size. You may really want a large dog, but if you live in an apartment or small house, that wouldn't be fair to the dog or yourself. On the same note, you may really want a small dog, but if you live on a property that has acres and acres of land, you may easily lose track of that dog. The ideal size of your dog should depend on your living situation. It is also a good idea to consider whether you will be moving within the next couple of years to ensure that you will be able to take your dog with you.

Age. What is the ideal age of a dog to you? Do you want a puppy, a middle-aged dog or a senior dog? A good way to decide this is to ask yourself how much time you want to commit. If you get a puppy, you will need to have enough time to dedicate to training and playing with it. On the other hand, if you adopt a middle-aged dog, you may not have to go through the training process. If you adopt an older dog, are you prepared to keep up with any health issues it may have?

Your Commitments. Do you work a lot or are you a "stay-at-home" person? Depending on how much time you'll be spending at home is important to consider when picking a dog. If you work a lot, you should consider not getting a dog that is high maintenance or clingy. If you absolutely must, you should also consider hiring help to take care of the dog while you are not at home.

Chapter 2: How To Care For Puppies

Picking between an adult dog and a puppy is another decision that requires some great consideration. Puppies often require some special care so this chapter will go over everything you need to know if you're thinking about getting a puppy.

Puppy Care Basics

When you bring your new puppy home, one of the first things you should do is show him the spot where he will be using the bathroom. After that, you can give it the grand tour of your home. If you have some toys, put them out to make it feel comfortable and at home. Using a leash, you can walk your puppy around the house and introduce it to each room. After your puppy gets used to its new home, it is important to jump right into training. There are many benefits to training your dog from a puppy.

Sleeping

When you first bring your puppy home, you should expect that it will spend the first few nights crying, especially after you've gone to sleep yourself. The reason a puppy cries is because it is experiencing separation. It has been separated from its mother and now it has been separated from you. Luckily, there are some things you can do for your puppy to help it transition into its new home.

Tire It Out. A good way to get your puppy to go right to sleep is to tire it out so it does not have the energy to stay up crying. A good way to execute this strategy is to feed your puppy early and then spend a few hours playing with it. This is to prevent your puppy from napping; otherwise it will be up all night—just like a baby. Right before you say goodnight to your puppy, make sure it goes to bathroom to avoid any accidents. Some experts believe that it is okay to allow your puppy to spend the night in your room to help it transition.

Help It Feel Close to Home. Experts also recommend helping your puppy feel close to home. A really good idea is to bring some old blankets to the breeder or farm where you're getting your puppy from and place it with its mother and litter. This way, you can bring home the scent of them with your puppy. To emulate the warmth of its mother and litter mates, you can wrap a hot water bottle with a towel and let your puppy snuggle with it at bedtime. Beware of letting your puppy sleep in your bed—if it gets too used to that, it may be hard to gather up some alone time for yourself. A good idea is to pick one area for your puppy and let it continue to sleep there.

- Never take out your frustration on a puppy; otherwise they will begin to see you in a negative light. There is a huge difference between a firm "no" and scaring the heck out of your new puppy.

- Do not allow your puppy to associate crying with attention; otherwise it will cry all the time when it wants something. Although it can be hard and tempting, try not to always run to him or her when it cries.

- Get your puppy in the habit of only going in your bed when you say it is okay. This helps the puppy understand that you're in charge.

Crate Training

Peoples' opinions on crate training can go either way. Some people are against it, noting that it can be cruel to your dog. Supporters of crate training believe that is a way to naturally allow your dog to find a safe space when it is nervous or scared. Some people also like to use it as a form of housebreaking.

The first step of crate training is to get a crate that is big enough to house your dog. A good rule of thumb in determining how big the crate should be is to add 3 inches to your dog's height and width. Keep in mind that your dog may grow.

The second step of crate training is to decide what kind of crate to buy. The main type of crates to choose from is wire, plastic and soft-sided crates. Wire crates create a sense of open space which can make the crate cooler. They are also easy to transport. Plastic crates look better than wire crates and are good for airport transportation. The one drawback of plastic crates is that your dog may get too hot or scared from the lack of open space. Soft-sided crates are like plastic crates except they are softer. The cons of these types of crates are that they are hard to clean if your dog accidentally goes in it and they tend to be more expensive.

The third step is to start the training process. The most important thing is to help your dog look at the crate in a positive light. If you get your dog into the habit of associating the crate with negativity, you can cause anxiety whenever you put the dog inside. Also, be sure to monitor how long your dog stays in the crate. You should never leave it inside for longer than a few hours at the max.

A good way to help your dog get used to the crate is to put its toys inside. You can also line it with a dog bed or comfortable blankets to make it more inviting. Allow your dog to go inside on its own. If your dog doesn't naturally take to the crate, another option is to put treats inside it to get your dog to go in. Never rush this process. A good idea is to leave a trail of treats to gradually help your dog go in.

Once your dog gets used to the crate, start putting its dish in there and let it eat. You can close the door the first time it eats inside, but make sure you open it right away when it is done. Then you can gradually leave the door closed for longer periods of time. Pay close attention to how your dog reacts and always make sure that you never scare or frighten it.

All in all, the most important parts about crate training are that you should never leave the dog locked in for long periods of time and you should never force the dog in. It is a process that may take some time depending on your dog, but as long as you patiently work with it, your dog should successfully get used to its crate.

Potty Training

Potty training your puppy as early as possible is important for preventing accidents, making it easier for your dog to relieve itself and making it much easier on you in the long run. Although many people dread potty training their puppy, it is actually quite easy.

Step 1: Pick a spot where your puppy will relieve itself. Make sure it is in a remote location, away from the places where people will be. Picking one specific location will make it easy for your dog to know where to go and easy for you when you have to clean up after it.

Step 2: Schedule a time when your dog will relieve itself. Try your best to schedule this in with its feeding time, playtime and sleep time. The better your time schedule, the easier it will be to prevent accidents.

Step 3: Feed your dog quality food because that will affect how much it goes to the bathroom. A high quality dog food often contains a lot of vitamins and minerals which will in turn create less waste.

Step 4: Have treats on hand, especially when you are training your puppy for the first time. A reward for good behavior can go a long way. Praise and rewards can serve as positive reinforcement, which will encourage your puppy to repeat the right behavior.

Step 5: Make sure everyone in your house follows the rules for potty training. If everyone has their own way of doing it, your dog may get confused and the process will take longer. Make sure everyone is consistent.

There are some other important things to consider when it comes to potty training. First, you should pay close attention to your dog's bathroom behaviors. If your dog does not follow a pattern or does not relieve itself at all, you should immediately consult with your vet. The first thing you should do when you bring your puppy home is put it on a leash and take it out to its "spot."

What If Your Puppy Has an Accident?

It is important to remember that accidents happen and it is very likely that your puppy may have an accident or two. The main thing to remember is to never, ever get mad or angry with your puppy. A good way to prevent accidents is to start noticing your puppy's signs that it needs to go. These signs commonly include whimpers or circling at the door.

If an accident does occur, take a deep breath and stay calm. If you have a crate, gently put your puppy inside or have another family member take it in the yard. Clean up the accident and avoid yelling or muttering in frustration. It is very important to clean up the spot thoroughly; otherwise your puppy may smell it later on and take it as a sign to go there again. A good way to ensure a proper cleaning is to use an enzymatic cleaner.

After you've cleaned up, take your puppy outside to make sure that is has fully relieved itself. If he goes in the right spot, make sure to praise it and give it a treat so it gets used to that area. Some other good ideas for avoiding accidents is to refrain from letting your puppy have water at night and take it out every 10 minutes after eating until it goes to the bathroom.

Chapter 3: Welcoming A New Dog Or Puppy Into Your Home

Whether you are bringing home a brand new puppy or adopting a middle-aged/senior dog, welcoming a dog into your home is a big, important step in the process. It's almost similar to bringing home a new baby—you have to make sure that you are 100% prepared and that your house is ready to become a home to a puppy or dog.. This chapter will help you discover everything you need to know about getting your home ready so you can bring home your newest best friend.

Getting Ready as Family

When you are getting ready to welcome a puppy or dog into your home, it is important that everyone in your household is on board. Everyone should be on the same page about how to treat and handle the dog as well as how to keep it on schedule and how to feed it. Don't be afraid to delegate some dog care tasks to your kids, either, as long as they understand the responsibility of it.

You and/or your partner should set aside some time to talk with your child/children about the importance of good behavior around the dog. By doing this before you actually bring the dog home, your children are more likely to be ready and prepared. Make sure that your children understand how a dog behaves. Explain to them that dogs perceive children in a different light than adults—to a dog, a child who is running around and waving their arms around may come off as a toy or prey and that could prompt the dog to bite. Also help them understand that grabbing the dog, even if meant for a hug, can come off as threatening. It is a good idea to always supervise your children and dogs until you have established a sense of trust and responsibility in both.

It is also a good idea to lay down ground rules before you actually bring the dog home. Figure out amongst your household who will be responsible for taking care of the dog at what times and hold everyone accountable for their responsibilities.

If you have other pets, you should plan a routine trip to the vet before your new dog arrives. This is just a preventative measure to make sure that none of your other pets are carrying any fleas or illnesses that your new dog can contract. If you have a female dog and are bringing home a male dog or vice-versa, you may want to talk to your vet about getting one fixed so you don't end up with more dogs than you bargained for.

Also, consider the behavior of your other pets as well as the behavior of the dog you're planning on bringing home. Some dogs get along well with both other dogs and cats but other times it can be a complete nightmare. Consider the temperament of each animal you have and ask yourself if you truly believe they could get along with another animal.

A good time to bring the dog home is on the weekend or another day where everyone in your family can be together at the same time. This way, everyone can get to know the dog at the same time and it gives you a few days to bond. With that being said; if you have other pets, try to make them feel included as well.

Inside Your House

Preparing the inside of your home for a new dog is very important. Make sure you have everything you need prepared ahead of time—toys, food, blankets, etc. Have your dog's sleeping area all set up in advance. Once you have that all set up, it is time to evaluate the rest of your home. Oh—don't forget your dog's collar with it's ID tags in case it gets out!

Slippery floors such as hardwood or linoleum can make it difficult for your dog to walk on. Slippery stairs are another thing to watch out for, especially if you're welcoming an older dog into your life. A good idea is to buy some cheap carpet and nail it to your stairs and lay it down anywhere else that your new dog may be exploring to make it easier on their legs and paws.

Dogs love to rub up against furniture, which can often cause wear over an extended period of time. A good way to prevent this is to purchase some cheap, washable furniture covers. Some dogs will figure out a way to open up cabinets in the kitchen or bathroom. A quick fix for this problem is to install some childproof locks on the doors. It may be a good idea to keep your trash cans locked behind a cabinet if it is small enough to fit. Finally, always keep your toilet lid down—enough said.

Make sure to keep your home clean and organized. Put away all shoes, socks, toys, wires, etc. that may pique your dog's interest. Most dogs love to chew and they don't care whether they're chewing on their own toys or on your favorite shoes. My friend had a beagle when she was little and she left her toys out one night. When she woke up the next day, she found one of her plastic dolls all chewed up. Not a happy morning for her.

With that being said, make sure that you don't leave food lying around in easy reach. Your dog will more than likely try to snatch it away given the chance and this can create poor habits as well as promote poor health. You should never allow your dog to eat human food, as some foods can contain poisonous ingredients to dogs (such as chocolate). However, just like we love to have the occasional treat, you can feed your dog human food every once in a awhile, as long as you know it is safe for your dog. Here is a good website to give you some ideas on safe human food for dogs: 39 everyday foods that are safe for dogs.

One thing you might want to consider investing in is a doggy door so that your dog can freely walk in and out of the house. This is good to have if you're going to be away at work for most of the day and you don't want to crate train your dog or leave it outside for too long. Doggy doors can often turn into stylish additions to your back doors. It also gives your dog the freedom to go to the bathroom whenever it chooses, freeing up your valuable time for other things.

Outside Your House

Evaluate the outside of your home as well as the inside. If you have a garden with lots of plants and flowers, it would be wise to research them and see if any may be toxic to your dog. The last thing that you want is your dog to get curious in the flower patch and then accidentally eat a poisonous flower. For a list of toxic plants to dogs, just click here. The same goes for fertilizer or pesticides on your garden or lawn—both are generally toxic to dogs. A good idea is to figure out a new way to keep your plants healthy that is not be harmful to another animals. Another option is to fence the garden in so that your dog cannot access it.

Be sure to keep all poisonous chemicals safely stored in a garage, shed, basement, or any other storage area that is out of your dog's reach. Also be sure to get rid of any standing water that you have lying around because it can contain harmful bacteria. Make sure that your car is not leaking oil or any other fluids if you keep it parked in the yard or garage.

Make sure that your backyard is fenced or gated. Be sure that the fence is strong, durable and does not have any holes or other means of escape. Double-check that the locks on the entry ways are working and cannot be pushed over. If you have a large dog, make sure that your fence is not short enough for your dog to jump over. Also ensure that your dog will not be able to dig its way under the fence.

If you have a pool or any other large source of water, make sure that it is secured by a gate. Some dogs love to swim and will jump right into the water but you don't want this to happen if you're not around. Another good idea for setting up your yard is to provide your dog with its own doghouse. Don't forget to clean it regularly. Finally, always keep your yard clean of feces, broken toys, or anything else that does not belong.

More Tips

If you're adopting a rescue dog, it is important to be patient and give your dog some time to get used to its new home. Given enough time, your dog will relax and begin to show its true personality. Before that occurs, however, it is important to never make your dog fearful, nervous, or anxious.

Similarly, if you're adopting a middle-aged dog, he or she might have some bad habits that have been carried over from the previous owners. If your dog does something undesirable, such as jump up on the furniture, never get angry or frustrated. Instead, be patient, gentle, and start working on re-training it.

Allow your dog to socialize with other people or animals. This can be healthy for your dog and promotes good behavior. As always, never force your dog to be in a situation that it doesn't like—if you sense that your dog will not get along with another person or animal, remove it from the situation.

Always present yourself as the leader!! Never let your dog think that it is the boss of you—*otherwise,* it will be impossible to get your dog under control if it gets unruly. It can be very embarrassing among your family and friends if they see your dog bossing you around.

Schedule regular appoints with your vet. If you don't have a vet, get one right away. Treat your dog as if it were another human—humans have regular doctor visits, so it is important for your dog to have its own doctor visits to.

Chapter 4: Proper Nutrition For Dogs And Puppies

If you haven't noticed already, your dog probably loves to eat! Dogs are like humans in that they need to balance their meals with their health. Dogs that have an irregular eating pattern or bad eating habits, like stealing table scraps, are less likely to live as long as dogs that have a good nutrition regime. Not only will providing your dog with top-notch nutrition help it live longer, but it can also help reduce any unnecessary vet bills that you may incur as a result of illness. This chapter will go over what you need to know for providing your dog with great, healthy meals.

First Things First...

First and foremost, your dog will need lots of water to stay hydrated. Many people think it is enough to just leave a water bowl out and let their dog drink from it whenever it needs. However, some dogs may under-drink while others may over-drink and this can lead to problems. Too much water can lead to a swollen stomach or even death by water toxicity. Too little water can lead to kidney stones, dehydration and sometimes even death. It is important to monitor and be knowledgeable of your dog's drinking habits.

A good way to determine how much water you can give your dog is to simply follow this equation: One half to one ounce of water times your dog's weight in pounds. So a dog that is 30 pounds should be drinking 15-30 ounces of water per day. Always provide your dog with water after exercise and be aware of the outside temperature. You can give your dog a little more water on those hot, summer days. Medications can also have an effect on your dog's water intake so always consult with your vet before making any changes.

How to check for dehydration: Gently grab a piece of your dog's skin on the back of its neck and pull it back. Let it go and notice how quickly it returns to its original form. If it quickly falls back into place, your dog is hydrated. If it moves slowly it can be a sign of dehydration. To confirm dehydration, take a look at your dog's gums. If they are sticky and dull, it is likely that your dog needs water.

What You Need To Know About Dog Food

Now that you know how to properly hydrate your dog, the next step is to get up to date on dog food. Dogs get their energy through their food, so it is important to feed them the highest quality food possible. High quality dog food is known to promote healthier coats, solid waste and good digestion.

Research has also found that the best dog foods have the ingredient "protein from meat" listed at the very top of the nutritional label. You should always read the nutrition labels on packages of dog food before giving it to your dog. Avoid dog food with ingredients such as corn flour or corn meal.

It is believed that human-grade dog food is the best kind that you can provide for your dog. This means that the food is good enough for humans to consume. Human-grade dog foods provide essential vitamins and minerals through meat, vegetable and whole grain sources. That's almost identical to the human diet. A lot of the big, name-brand dog food manufacturers use low-grade meats that are comprised of animal parts, which is neither healthy for dogs or humans. Commercial dog foods that are marketed as "premium" are usually the best out of all the big-name dog food companies.

There are three main types of dog food: dry, packaged and semi-moist. Some companies also manufacture all-natural dog food. You can usually distinguish this by reading the labels but the colors on this type of packaging tend to be earth-like. Finally, although there is currently little research or evidence to support it, some experts believe that a raw food diet can be really good.

Many dog owners prefer dry dog food because it is easy to store, easy to serve and easy to buy. It is important to pay attention to the labels if you are going to provide dry food to your dog. Dry food that is cheaper tends to be made from low-grade ingredients but there are options out there that are made with high-quality, organic ingredients. One good thing about dry dog food is that some are vegetable-based. So if your dog happens to have an allergy to meat, you could provide it with this type of food.

Organic dog food is slowly gaining popularity among some dog owners. Organic dog foods are made with all-natural meat and grain sources, making them of much higher quality than other foods. Most organic dog foods also contain vegetable extracts, which serve as the main source of vitamins and minerals. Although organic dog food will definitely run higher in terms of costs, the benefits are worth it. The ingredients in organic dog food are everything that your dog needs to stay healthy and functioning. It's also really good for dogs with food allergies.

Things You Should Never Feed Your Dog...

Some people mistake "human-grade food" for being *anything*. However, some human foods can be dangerous and harmful to your dog's health so it is important to only feed them dog food for the most part. Certain human foods can kill your dog. Though the list of things that can be dangerous for your dog are things you probably wouldn't feed it anyway, it is good to know in the back of your head because you can keep those items out of your dog's reach. Never feed your dog apple seeds, coffee beans, avocados, salt, garlic, grapes, nuts, chocolate, or candy. It is also important to keep artificial sweeteners, alcohol, soda or tea away from your dog's reach. These food items can cause everything from diarrhea to paralysis to death. Check out this YouTube video by Food Farmer Earth for some safe human foods for dogs: Healthy Foods to Feed Your Dog.

How to Pick the Right Dog Food

With the tremendous selection of dog foods on the market, it can be an overwhelming decision to figure out what type of dog food you should buy. Knowing that human-grade is the best, there are still options. As you have learned from a previous chapter, there are many different breeds of dogs, all of which have different health and nutritional needs. There is no "one-size-fits-all" when it comes to picking out the right food for your dog. Here are some things to consider:

How old is your dog? Puppies will always have a different diet than older dogs. Most dog foods lists the appropriate age range on their packaging so be sure to pay attention.

How is your dog's health? Remember how important it is to monitor and take care of your dog's health? If your dog has a condition that requires it to eat a special diet, than you will really have to pay attention to what you're serving up. Many manufacturers make foods that are aimed at dogs with special diets so a good place to start would be to find out those brands.

What is your budget? Consider this question carefully. It is ideal to not sacrifice the quality of your dog's food to save yourself money, over the long haul; you can actually save a lot of money in vet bills with good food and also have a happier, healthier and longer living dog as a bonus.

Dry vs Canned Food

You already know the pros and cons of dry dog food. Canned dog food can be just fine for your dog as long as you know which ones to avoid. As you discovered earlier, you should always look for "protein from meat" as the first ingredient on the label. Additionally, look to see if the label lists specific meats and not just something generic like "other meat sources." Go for canned foods that have a high percentage of specific meat products (at least 65%). Another thing to avoid in canned foods is sugar and gluten. As you know, sugar can go as far as to kill your dog. One thing that you *should* look for is sources from vegetables and whole grains.

Also, be sure to remember that a diet of canned food and fresh foods can lead to a much higher rate of tooth decay unless other precautions are made. Dogs with a high dry dog food content will tend to have healthier teeth for a much longer time.

When in Doubt...

When in doubt about picking the right food for you dog, one thing you can always rely on is customer reviews. Go to Amazon.com or the website of your local pet store and see what other people are saying about the brand you're thinking about getting. Most people are specific in their reviews (such as, "I bought this food for my 1 year old beagle...) so it can be really easy to find the answers to your questions by doing this. You can also see if there's anyone at the pet store that you can stop and talk to for advice.

Chapter 5: Playtime For Dogs And Puppies

Dogs are well-known for their love to play, whether it is playing catch, tug of war, or "chase-me-around-the-yard." It is very important to play with your dog, especially if he or she is energetic. Playtime helps stimulate your dog's mind, which in turn can keep them out of trouble (like going through the garbage or drinking out of the toilet). Dogs that are fast learners are the ones who are most likely to grow bored the fastest. Playtime also helps keep your dog's mentality sharp and it promotes good socialization skills. Finally, playing with your dog together as a couple or family is some great bonding time for all.

You should note that dogs learn how to play from each other. If your dog is not playful, you may need to teach it how to play. This won't be a hard task at all as long as you don't mind acting like a dog for a little while! Dogs learn best by using body language, so you will literally have to act like a dog—you'll have to get down on your hands and knees, bow, and even bark to get your dog's attention. Bounce yourself up and down and bark some more. If your dog barks back at you, get up, walk away, and then come back and repeat the process. After a while your dog should get into the groove of "playtime."

Dog Playtime Favorites

Chase the Toy. Dogs love to chase. Since you're the leader, don't get your dog into the habit of chasing you or it may think everything is a game. Instead, use a dog toy, an old sock, or something that is safe for your dog to have in its mouth. More often than not you can just keep throwing your dog's favorite toy around and let it run with it until it tires out and brings it back to you.

Hide and Seek. You can play hide and seek with your dog just like as if you were playing with another human. Hide somewhere easy at first, somewhere obvious like behind the couch, and call your dog into the room. When it finds you, praise it well and maybe even give it a treat. Once your dog masters finding you in the easy spots you can make it a bit more challenging.

Soccer. Teaching your dog how to play soccer is very easy. First, start by slowly kicking a ball along the ground toward your dog. Let it go after the ball and once it figures out it can't pick it up by its teeth, it will get the hang of nudging it with its nose or paws. Praise your dog every time you see it getting into the game. When your dog has really mastered soccer you can add another human to make the game more fun.

Find It. This short and simple game is a good way to help your dog practice its focus abilities. Simply have your dog sit and wave your hand under its nose while you're holding a treat. Let your dog sniff the treat and then hide it somewhere simple (a good idea is to put it under a towel) and tell your dog to find it. When it finds the treat, don't forget to give praise! You can make the game harder and harder as your dog gets used to finding it in easy places.

Obstacle Course. Clear out your living room or use a big room where your dog won't run into anything valuable or harmful. Get some old blankets and pillows and strategically place them on the floor, creating an "obstacle course." Walk your dog through it a few times and then place it at the beginning and call it. See how long it takes your dog to get through the obstacle course by itself.

Tug of War. This game is the favorites of many. Some people argue against tug of war, saying that it can bring out aggression in already-aggressive dogs. However, when done right, this game can actually help your dog release aggression and it can serve as a learning lesson to "let go." Get your dog into the habit of not grabbing the other end of the rope until you give the signal. When you're done, get your dog into the habit of letting it go when you say so. Have plenty of praises and treats on hand to reward good behavior associated with this game.

Frisbee. Dogs commonly chase after balls, but have you ever considered using a Frisbee instead? Frisbee can be a little more challenging for a dog because it moves faster and flies higher. It's a great way to help your dog practice its focus and concentration skills.

Stay, Come. This simple game is a good one for young kids and parents to play with the dog. It's similar to the traditional "Red Light/Green Light" kid's game. Instead of yelling red light or green light, you can substitute those words for "stay" or "come." Have your young child and dog play at the same time and see who can listen best.

Practice Commands. Although training can seem like something more serious than a game, you can actually turn it into a game by practicing it with your dog. Think of it as a doggie version of "Simon Says."

Videos

The Shell Scent Game by Donna Hill teaches your dog to find and paw to indicate a scent.

The Muffin Tin Game by Donna Hill builds problem-solving skills and stimulates dogs.

Everything You Need to Know to Teach Your Dog a Perfect Fetch posted by Zak George's Dog Training rEvolution.

Chapter 6: How to Train Your Dog Or Puppy

Dogs are different from cats not only in their size, breeds and interests, but also because they have a powerful ability to learn. While it is possible to train your cat, it is much more common and easier to train your dog. Though it is easier to train a dog than a cat, it is important to remember that training your dog will take some time, patience and dedication and remember that it will not happen overnight.

While many people just pay for their dog to go to "school" where a professional trainer can teach them everything they need to know, it is possible (and cheaper) to train your dog yourself at home. Training your dog at home also allows the opportunity for you and your dog to bond together.

The Behavior of Your Dog

Understanding how and why your dog behaves is the first thing you need to do before you actually jump into the training process.

Does your dog circle its sleeping area before laying down? You may notice that your dog will sometimes circle the area it's going to sleep in before laying down. This is a natural instinct that dogs have because they believe it makes their sleeping area softer.

Does your dog blink? This question may arise as strange, as blinking comes to humans naturally. However, it is a little different in dogs. Dogs only blink when their brains are processing information. This commonly occurs when you command your dog to do something. Next time you do, watch your dog's eyes—if he or she blinks, you can be sure that your dog understands you.

Does your dog grunt or wine? You may notice your dog grunting or whining. A grunt from a dog is a good sign, as it shows that the dog is happy. On the other hand, a whine often shows that your dog is lacking something important. Dogs usually whine when they are lonely, hungry, or cold.

Does your dog walk away when you try to pet it? You may notice that your dog will lose interest in you if you try to pet them. This may leave you feeling hurt and confused. Pay attention to the way you pet your dog. If you're patting you're dog on the head briskly, you're actually giving off the sense that you're being dominant, even though you might just be trying to love your dog. A better way to give your dog affection is to stroke it instead of patting it. Dogs like to be stroked on the face and in the front of their bodies. Some also like to be stroked on the top of their bodies near their tail.

Some Of The Best Training Techniques For Your Puppy or Dog

Now it is time to learn some of the best methods for learning how to properly train your dog. This section will start off with how to teach your dog basic commands, as those are the most important. (sit, stay, heel, etc). Once your dog has mastered the basic commands, you can then move on to teach it tricks. One important thing to note is that many people believe that you should spend a lot of time training your dog, but that is actually not true. Research shows that the best way to train your dog is to really focus on the final result and try to achieve it within 10-15 minutes. For example, if you're going to teach your dog how to "stay," you should try to get your dog to master it within that time frame.

Stay. Stay is a common command that is good for teaching your dog to stand in place. It is useful for when you do not want your dog to follow you, such as when you are going to walk out the door to go to work. It can also help you control your dog when you have friends, family, or guests over. Here is a good technique that you can use to help your dog learn this command:

Step 1: Put a collar and leash on your dog and sit next to it. Spread your fingers out in a "stop" motion with your hand and put it in front of your dog's nose while firmly saying, "Stay."

Step 2: Move in front of your dog and stand there for a few minutes before moving back to your sitting position. If your dog listens, be sure to give it a treat and pet it while saying positive things. "Your such a good doggie!"

Step 3: If your dog does not listen, gently say "No" and keep trying.

Step 4: Once your dog has mastered the stay command, work on teaching it a word that will let it know it is okay to move again, such as "Go."

A good idea is to slowly increase the distance between you and your dog as you practice. This helps your dog truly understand the point of this command. Stay where your dog can see you the first few times, but you will soon be able to leave the room. If you want to know whether your dog has mastered this command or not, you could use some toys as a distraction to see if it is working. Also, be sure to practice this in a fenced area if you're going to do it outside.

To see the process of this command visually, check out this YouTube video by Zak George's Dog Training rEvolution, Dog Training 101: How to Teach Your Dog to Stay (Duration).

Down. Down is an important command for preventing your dog from jumping on things or people. The only downside to teaching this command is that it can tend to be submissive, so your dog may not be as willing to cooperate with you. A good idea is to use a happy attitude and a handful of treats to help your dog master this command.

Step 1: Put a treat in your hand and wrap it in your palm. Put your palm near the dog's nose and allow it to become aware of the treat.
Step 2: Slowly move your hand toward the floor. Your dog should follow it.
Step 3: Bring your hand across the floor, which should prompt your dog to stretch its body out. Once your dog gets into that position, allow it to have the treat and do the usual praising.
Step 4: Practice this a few times a day until your dog is successful.

Never force or push your dog down—instead, wait for it to lie down on its own and reward it while repeating the word "Down."

Come. Come is a good command for learning how to get your dog away from trouble or if you just want it to come over to you on command. While this is an easy command to teach, it sometimes requires a little bit of patience. Here is a great way to teach this to your dog:

Step 1: Put a collar on your dog and attach a leash to it and let the dog walk around on its own for a few minutes.

Step 2: Grab a few treats and then take the leash in your hands.

Step 3: Let the dog continue to lead the way for a few minutes and then start walking in the opposite direction.

Step 4: Wait until your dog starts to follow you and repeat the words "come," slowly while giving him a treat and positive reinforcement.

Step 5: Practice learning this command a few times a day until your dog has mastered it.

Don't use this command in a scary or angry voice and don't use it to get your dog to come to you for things such as a bath or a punishment. Also, don't chase after your dog if he or she runs away from you, otherwise it may think you are playing with them.

To see the process of this command visually, check out this YouTube video by Training Positive: How To Train Your Dog: "Come Here!" Perfectly!!!

Heel. Teaching your dog the command "Heel" is important for helping your dog learn how to walk on a leash properly. Doing this can help your dog quickly, easily and confidently navigate while being in the lead. This process will take some time and practice but it is an important command for your dog to know.

Step 1: Start by having your dog stand to the left of you.

Step 2: Put some treats into your left hand and put it in front of your dog's nose.

Step 3: Say the command "Walk," and begin heading forward.

Step 4: As your dog walks alongside you at the same pace, give your dog a treat every few steps. If your dog pulls ahead or to the side, stop giving it treats. Command your dog to sit and then start over by putting more treats into your hand and waving them under your dog's nose again.

Step 5: Practice this for about a week, gradually increasing the number of steps you take until your dog masters it. As your dog begins to catch on, only reward it after every couple of steps instead of every step.

To see the process of this command visually, check out this YouTube Video: How To Train A Dog To Heel by Dog Training by K9-1.com.

Sit. Sit is one of the easier and most basic commands that you can help your dog learn. Training your dog to sit can help you control your dog better and prevent it from jumping on your friends, family, or guests. Here is a really great, easy, and effective technique for training your dog to sit:

Step 1: Take a treat in your hand and sit on a chair with your dog next to you.

Step 2: Let your dog smell the treat in your hand so they become aware of it. Then, raise it slightly (not too high but not low enough for the dog to grab it). Repeat the word "sit."

Step 3: Slowly raise your hand with the treat until the dog naturally sits down. When you see them sit, allow them to have the treat and give them some positive reinforcement, such as petting them while saying, "Good boy/girl!"

Step 4: Practice this command with your dog several times a day until they get it down.

If your dog does not sit on its own, you can gently push it into the sitting position. Another good strategy is to watch your dog. Whenever it sits on its own, you can reward it with positive reinforcement. Good places to practice this training include in front of its bowl and near your front entrance, as your dog will then be able to practice "good manners."

To see the process of this command visually, check out this YouTube video: How To Teach Your Dog To Sit posted by Howcast.

The Emergency Call. Teaching your dog an emergency call is very important because it could save your dog's life in a dangerous situation. This command should only be used in life threatening situations, like if your dog is sitting in the middle of a street and there's heavy traffic. That being said, it is important to have this command on hand to ensure the safety of your dog at all times.

Step 1: Pick a unique word that you wouldn't normally use in everyday life.

Step 2: Use a very special treat, something that your dog will just come running for. Good examples are lunch meat or a hot dog...again something you normally wouldn't feed your dog but you know it would devour.

Step 3: Practice the command in a small area to start. Yell the command word in a high-pitched, positive voice. Do whatever it takes to get your dog's attention—show it the treats, pat your legs, anything.

Step 4: As soon as your dog comes over to you, give it the treats and praise it highly. Have enough treats on hand for 20 seconds and let your dog go crazy.

Step 5: Make sure that your dog goes back to its original activity or it will not make a connection with the command.

Step 6: Practice this trick once or twice a day in the small area you've selected.

Step 7: When your dog masters this skill in the small area, gradually begin to move to a bigger area but continue to feed it the same type of treats each time.

Note: Never use this emergency command in a non-emergency situation. It may be tempting to use when your dog is not listening to you but if you overuse the command, it may not work in true emergencies.

To see the process of this command visually, check out this YouTube video by rogersmmr: Teach Your Dog To Come (Recall Training).

Chapter 7: How to Keep Dogs And Puppies Healthy

Last but certainly not least, it is very important that you keep your dog healthy. Keeping your dog in good health can mean a longer lifespan, less vet bills and a much happier dog. You already know the importance of providing your dog with a healthy diet and regular exercise, but there are some other aspects of health that are important, too. It is your responsibility to keep your dog healthy. Since it can't directly say to you, "Hey, I think I have [insert ailment here]," knowing your dog and understanding its behavior is a must. That way, when you notice it acting differently, you have a sign that you may need to take it to the vet.

Here's how to tell if your dog is generally healthy:

Check your dog's skin. Make sure that it is smooth and without scabs, flakes, or any other abnormalities. You can check for fleas or other parasites by brushing its hair back and looking for moving black specs. Next, look at your dog's coat. It should be smooth and shiny. Look for any excess oiliness or bald spots. A healthy dog's eyes should be shiny and clear. Make sure that the whites of its eyes are not tinted yellow. Its ears should be clean and pink on the insides. Look out for excess wax (a little wax is normal) and redness. Generally, signs of a healthy dog's nose include: coolness and dampness. Finally, check your dog's mouth. Its gums should be pink and firm. Some dog's gums may be black or spotted.

Skin Diseases.

It is important to pay attention to how much your dog scratches itself. Mild scratching is normal but if your dog seems to get itchy a lot, it could mean several things. Some of the most common reasons for excessive scratching are fleas, allergies, fungal infections, or bacterial infections. Skin problems make up a high number of reasons as to why dogs are taken to the vet. A common indicator of allergies is when your dog constantly licks its paws or rubs its nose in your rug.

A good way to determine whether your dog has an allergy is to have its blood tested. You can also try a few home remedies to stop the allergies yourself. You can try to give your dog a bath in colloidal oatmeal shampoo once a week. You can also add fatty acid supplements to its food, which may help stop itching.

Bacterial infections can often be identified by looking for sores, scabs, or pimples on your dog's skin. Antibiotics are usually the best method of treatment. Fungal infections can be identified by looking for red, oozing sores on your dog's paws or in between skin folds. These infections can usually be treated with medical baths and anti-fungal medications.

To determine if your dog is itchy from fleas or other skin parasites, I would suggest investing in a flea comb. Use the comb to inspect your dog's hair for fleas or little specs known as flea dirt. Also, pay close attention to the tail area, as that's where fleas like to hang out. Personally, fleas are one of the top two things I would like to be extinct on this planet! Be sure to look out for ticks as well, which can be dangerous because they transmit harmful diseases, such as Lyme disease.

You can treat fleas by bathing your dog with a special shampoo or spray. You should also machine wash everything you can in your house and give the floors a good vacuum. A good idea is to put some boric acid on your carpets and vacuum after an hour. The boric acid kills fleas and their larvae, making them easier to eliminate. To treat ticks, carefully inspect your dog for them and use tweezers to remove. Afterward, clean the infected area with gentle soap and water and keep an eye on it for a few days to make sure it's not infected or irritated. A good way to prevent fleas and ticks in the first place is to invest in a special collar that will help prevent them. However, the best way that I have found, although a bit expensive, is Frontline Flea medicine! With all the pets I have had in my life... I can assure you, you do not want fleas to get in your carpet and become a nuisance! It gives me shudders thinking of all those ankle biting, blood sucking little nightmares that have gotten me over the years. That's why I make prevention a supremely high priority!

Digestive Problems.

When you get a dog, prepare to deal with diarrhea and vomiting, two of the most common digestive problems. Most often, digestive problems are not life-threatening and can be treated by you.

Know when you have a digestive problem on hand that is considered an emergency. Take your dog to the vet immediately if his sides or stomach look swollen, if it has eaten something that may get caught in its stomach (usually rope, cloth, or something else that can easily get stuck), if its vomit or feces has blood in it, or if it is too weak to walk. Don't hesitate to call your vet if you're not sure.

If your dog is just suffering from a regular case of diarrhea, there are some steps that you can take to treat it at home. First, only give it water for 12-24 hours after it starts showing signs. After that period, feed your dog a mixture of cooked rice and boiled chicken in small amounts, 3 times a day, for 3 days. If you see an improvement after 3 days, start mixing its regular food into the mixture. Gradually balance it out for another 3 days until your dog is eating its regular food again.

Diarrhea can often be caused by stress, usually if you go on vacation and leave your dog for a few days. The best way to prevent stress-induced diarrhea is to make sure that everything stays the same while you're gone. Give your dog's caretaker instructions on how to keep its feeding on schedule with the same food it's used too. Make sure your dog gets in the amount of exercise and playtime as usual and if possible, let it play with other neighborhood dogs.

If your dog is throwing up and it doesn't contain blood or any weird colors and it is not exhibiting any abnormal behavior, there is also a way you can treat it without having to go to the vet. Don't give your dog anything—food or water—for 12 hours since it last started throwing up. Don't worry about dehydration, as that won't happen after 12 hours as long as your dog is older and otherwise healthy. After the 12 hours, you can start to give your dog small doses of water. If it hasn't thrown up after a half hour, give your dog a little more water than you did the first time. After an hour, give your dog a mixture of cooked rice and boiled chicken in small amounts. If all goes well, give your dog small amounts of water and the mixture every 3 hours. After three days, begin mixing its regular food in with the mixture and gradually increase it until your dog is eating its regular food again.

If your dog has persistent digestive problems, it may be a sign of something more serious, such as nutritional deficiencies or chronic diseases.

Urinary Tract Infection.

A urinary tract infection is a common illness in dogs. It causes your dog to pee more than usual and many people mistake it for a behavioral problem. A good way to determine if your dog has a UTI is to be aware of its urination habits. A dog with a UTI often pees in the house even though it's trained not too. Also look out for excessive urination and an increase in thirst. A UTI in a dog is often caused by a bacterial infection in the urethra. Since a UTI treatment requires the use of antibiotics, there's not really much you can do to treat your dog at home. A trip to the vet usually ensues when you're dealing with a UTI.

Heartworm Disease

Heartworm disease is common in dogs and is caused by a parasite called Dirofilaria immitis, usually transmitted through mosquitos, probably my most second hated organism on this planet. This parasite can be fatal as it will attack your dog's heart and lungs. Although heartworm disease is common it is easily preventable.

Unfortunately, it can be hard to tell if your dog has heartworm disease until it has already developed into an advanced stage. The earliest sign of a mild heartworm is coughing. It is only until the heartworm is more severe that is causes more recognizable signs, such as breathing problems and stomach swelling. If you notice your dog coughing, you should consult with your vet to catch a heartworm in its earliest form. The best way to prevent heartworm disease is to make annual visits to your vet. Your vet can tell you more about heartworm disease and make recommendations based off the breed and type of your dog. Although heartworm disease preventative measures may cost a little more money, it is **very** important.

Dental Health

Many people overlook the importance of their dog's dental health. The truth is that a buildup of plaque can lead to some pretty serious health issues down the road. Good ways to help your dog practice good dental health is to brush its teeth regularly. You can also buy treats that are designed for optimum dental care. It may be a good idea to talk to your vet about professional cleaning if your dog's dental health is not up to par. Dry dog food is also helpful in preventing tooth decay.

Ear Infections.

Ear infections that go untreated can cause serious damage to your dog's ears. You can usually tell if your dog has an ear infection if it is shaking its head and scratching its ears a lot. There may also be discharge noticeable. If an ear infection lingers for more than two days, it is important to consult your vet, but there are some things you can do to treat it at home first.

Place your dog in the tub and lift up both its ears. Squirt some vet-approved ear cleanser on the inner flap of your dog's ear, close to its actual opening. Carefully place the tip of the bottle in your dog's ear opening and slowly squirt some inside. Quickly begin massaging the base of your dog's ear so that the cleanser works to loosen any debris. Once you're done massaging, you can let your dog shake its head out. Next, use a cotton swab or ball to clean out the ear canal. Don't forget to reward your dog with a treat afterward, as this can be a difficult, uncomfortable process.

Arthritis

Arthritis works just the same in dogs as it does in humans—it involves the inflammation of the joints and can be very painful. The most common types of arthritis in dogs include osteoarthritis, rheumatoid arthritis, and infective arthritis. Osteoarthritis is the most common type found in dogs. Unfortunately, there is no cure for osteoarthritis, but there are some things you can do to treat it.

The best way to prevent osteoarthritis is to watch your dog's diet. Obesity can put a strain on your dog's joints and bones so by helping your dog maintain a healthy weight, you can essentially slow the onset of osteoarthritis and make it less painful if your dog develops it. You can also keep your dog active to prevent stiffness. Another idea to help lessen joint pain is to invest in an orthopedic dog bed, which is great for providing comfort to painful joints. Finally, if you have hardwood floors, it may be difficult for your dog to walk on them so you may want to lay down some carpets, rugs, or anything else that will create some traction. As always, consult with your vet for more treatment options.

If you are not sure whether your dog may be suffering from osteoarthritis, look out for some common signs. Generally, your dog will be less likely to climb stairs or jump. It may be difficult to sit or stand. You may notice that your dog is no longer interested in playing or exercising and that it may be licking its joints more than usual. Your dog may sleep more than usual and it can tend to withdraw from you and your family members. The best way to know for sure is to schedule an evaluation with your vet. You can also try some joint medication such as: Sergeant's Vetscription Joint-Eze Plus Chewables Dog.

The Importance of Regular Vet Visits

As a part of keeping your dog in good health, it is important to schedule regular visits to your vet. This is not only a part of a preventative health plan but your vet will also be able to administer the vaccinations that your dog needs to stay healthy. Your vet can also spay or neuter your dog if you conclude that it would be for the best. Your vet will be able to check your dog for any common problems and he or she may catch a serious illness before it gets out of control.

Conclusion

Picking, training and taking care of a dog or puppy requires a lot of time, consideration, research and responsibility. Although dogs are pets that are the most similar to humans, it is still important to know about the proper nutrition and care for them. It is also important to play with your dog regularly and help it get some exercise so it lives a long, healthy life. Training your dog is important for being able to bring it around other people and for being able to stay in control.

I hope this book was able to help you to become more knowledgeable about dogs and dog care. If you have not yet picked a dog or puppy out yet, hopefully this book was able to give you more insight on each breed and what kind may be right for you. If you've already got your dog, I hope this book was able to help you learn about the best ways to play with, feed, and take care of your dog in terms of health, socialization, and training.

The next step is to think about what you're going to do to take care of your dog. Before you start anything, the best thing you can do is begin training your dog if you haven't already. A well-trained dog is always easier to work with when it comes to feeding, grooming, bathing, playing, etc. Once you've mastered training, you can begin to rethink your dog's diet, playtime and habits so that you can both share a great life together!

Finally, if you discovered at least one thing that has helped you or that you think would be beneficial to someone else, be sure to take a few seconds to easily post a quick positive review. As an author, your positive feedback is desperately needed. Your highly valuable five star reviews are like a river of golden joy flowing through a sunny forest of mighty trees and beautiful flowers! *To do your good deed in making the world a better place by helping others with your valuable insight, just leave a nice review.*

My Other Books and Audio Books
www.AcesEbooks.com

Peak Performance Books

Health Books

ULTIMATE HEALTH SECRETS

HEALTH

Strategies For Dieting, Eating Healthy, Exercising, Losing Weight, The Mediterranean Diet, Strength Training, And All About Vitamins, Minerals, And Supplements

Ace McCloud

ENERGY
ULTIMATE ENERGY

Discover How To Increase Your Energy Levels Using The Best All Natural Foods, Supplements And Strategies For A Life Full Of Abundant Energy

Ace McCloud

RECIPE BOOK

The Best Food Recipes That Are Delicious, Healthy, Great For Energy And Easy To Make

Ace McCloud

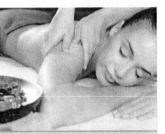

MASSAGE THERAPY

TRIGGER POINT THERAPY
ACUPRESSURE THERAPY
Learn The Best Techniques For Optimum Pain Relief And Relaxation

Ace McCloud

Be sure to check out my audio books as well!

Check out my website at: www.AcesEbooks.com for a complete list of all of my books and high quality audio books. I enjoy bringing you the best knowledge in the world and wish you the best in using this information to make your journey through life better and more enjoyable! **Best of luck to you!**

CPSIA information can be obtained
at www.ICGtesting.com
Printed in the USA
LVOW09*0636240418
574636LV00006BA/38/P